Meet Moses

Mortimer Borne

Meet Moses

Meet Moses

Fifty-four Drawings

YESHIVA UNIVERSITY
MUSEUM

ABARIS BOOKS

PUBLIC COLLECTIONS

OWNING EXAMPLES OF BORNE'S WORKS

Metropolitan Museum of Art

British Museum

Houston Museum of Fine Arts

Library of Congress

Smithsonian Institution

National Gallery of Art

New York Public Library

Boston Public Library

Bar - Ilan University

Israel Museum, Jerusalem

Municipal Museum of Ramat-Gan

University of Judaism Museum

First published by Abaris Books, Inc.
24 West 40th Street, New York, N.Y.10018

Printed in the U.S.A.
ISBN   0-913870-39-0
LC: 77-074180

CONTENTS

DRAWINGS   *Page*

Preface   7
Prologue: Labors of the Hebrews   9
The Finding of Moses   11
Miriam Suggests a Nurse   13
The Hebrew Nurse   15
Moses Tramples Pharaoh's Crown   17
Moses and Pharaoh's Daughter   19
Moses Visits His Family   21
Moses Invents a Stratagem   23
The Siege of the Ethiopian Capital   25
The Overseer Beaten   27
At the Well of Jethro   29
Jethro's Seven Daughters   31
Moses Tends the Flock of Jethro   33
The Burning Bush   35
Journey to Egypt   37
The Hebrews Forced to Gather Straw   39
And God Spake unto Moses   41
Moses Warns Pharaoh   43
Aaron's Rod Turns into a Serpent   45
The Plague of Frogs   47
The Plague of Lice   49
Rain of Hail   51
Darkness over Egypt   53
Moses and Aaron Address the Israelites   55
Exodus from Egypt   57
Drowning of the Egyptians   59
Song of Victory   61
Miriam and the Women Celebrate   63
Moses and the People at Marah   65
Quails Arrive for Sustenance   67
The Striking of the Rock   69
The Raised Hands of Moses   71
Revenge on the Amalekites   73

Jethro Advises Moses to Choose Judges   75
Moses Ascends Mount Sinai   77
God Spake all these Words   79
Moses Brings the Law   81
The Choosing of the Priests   83
Aaron as High Priest   85
Bezaleel Creates Works in Metal, Stone and Wood   87

The Golden Calf   89
Moses Breaks the Tablets   91
The Laws Brought Again   93
Moses Speaks to the Children of Israel   95
Revolt Against Moses   97
The Demise of Korah and His Men   99
Balaam and the Ass   101
The Daughters of Moab   103
Moses Turns Over the Command to Joshua   105
Moses and Joshua   107
Moses Beholds the Land of Canaan   109
Death of Moses   111
Epilogue: Fall of the Walls of Jericho   112

FOREWORD

Inspite of the advent of a burgeoning technology, of computerized data, and the discovery of the awesome power in nuclear explosions—the significance of human life, and the joys and pains that it entails, have not appreciably changed in the last 4000 years. The giant step forward, from barbarism and Gods with local jurisdictions, to the concept of a Universal God of all creation, as formulated by Moses, supercedes all other changes in the evolving history of man. All relevant social and religious movements in our day are like sonar echoes of the voice of Moses which spelled out the potentialities and limitations of human behavior.

Cognizant of the universality of the yearnings of the human spirit, artists of all eras have been fascinated and inspired by the Bible. In this series of drawings on the life of Moses, I was impelled to devise a special technique that I hoped would recall the spirit of the words of the Bible. As for the choice of incidents in the life of Moses, I limited myself to the five books of Moses and some events narrated by Flavius Josephus in his "Antiquities of the Jews," those that fill in some years in the life of Moses not mentioned in the Bible.

In retelling the story of Moses, which deals with specific characters in specific situations, I was compelled to employ the relatively figurative idiom as the only way in which the story can be told meaningfully in graphic visualization. I reserve the use of the abstract idiom wherever the personal abstraction can adequately express the concept.

My motivation for creating this series of drawings on the life of Moses is in response to a growing need and a great hunger in our day for some positive values to live by, for which the remembrance of Moses can serve as a guiding light.

Mortimer Borne
Nyack, New York 1978

PROLOGUE: LABORS OF THE HEBREWS

The curtain rises at a period when the benevolent and cooperative spirit between the Hebrews and the Egyptians, under the aegis of Joseph, deteriorated over the centuries, and there arose a king "who knew not Joseph." This king and his cabinet of priests were alarmed by the growing power of the Hebrews in numbers and in wealth and so connived in many ways to oppress them. The adult population of the Hebrews were enslaved and cruelly dealt with. They were forced to do hard labor and to build for Pharaoh treasure cities, Pithom and Ramses. . . .

To reduce the number of the Hebrew population, the Egyptians adopted a form of genocide: every male child born to the Hebrews was to be killed.

To Amram and Jochebed of the tribe of Levi a male child was born. To save the child's life they hid him for three months and then placed him in a waterproofed basket of reeds on the waters of the Nile.

THE FINDING OF MOSES

Now the daughter of Pharaoh came down to wash herself at the river . . . and when she saw the basket among the bulrushes she sent her maid to fetch it.

And when she saw the child, behold, the babe wept. And she had compassion on him, and said: This is one of the Hebrews' children.

MIRIAM SUGGESTS A NURSE

*Then said his sister to Pharaoh's daughter: Shall
I go and call a nurse of the Hebrew women, that she
may nurse the child for you?*

*And Pharaoh's daughter said to her: Go. And
the maid went and called the child's mother.*

THE HEBREW NURSE

And Pharaoh's daughter said to the Hebrew nurse: Take this child away, and nurse it for me, and I will give you your wages. And the woman took the child, and nursed it.

MOSES TRAMPLES PHARAOH'S CROWN

*Pharaoh's daughter put the infant Moses into
her father's hands; so he took him, and hugged him
close to his breast. And on his daughter's account,
in a pleasant way, put his diadem upon his head. But
Moses threw it down to the ground, and in a puerile
mood he wreathed it round, and tread upon it with
his feet. Now, this seemed to bring along with it an
evil presage concerning the kingdom of Egypt.*

MOSES AND PHARAOH'S DAUGHTER

*And the child grew, and the Hebrew nurse
brought him to Pharaoh's daughter, and he became
her son. And she named him Moses and said: Because
I drew him out of the water.*

MOSES VISITS HIS FAMILY

*And it came to pass in those days when Moses
was grown, he went out unto his brethren . . . .*

MOSES INVENTS A STRATAGEM

Moses as general of the Egyptian armies, while fighting the Ethiopians, invented a stratagem.

He made baskets of sedge and filled them with Ibis birds.

As soon as Moses and the army came to the ground which was difficult to be passed over because of multitude of serpents, the Ibis were let loose and repelled the serpents.

THE SIEGE OF THE ETHIOPIAN CAPITAL

Tharbis, daughter of the king of the Ethiopians, happened to see Moses as he led the army near to the walls. She admired the subtlety of his undertakings and fell deeply in love with him.

Upon the persistence of that passion, she sent to him the most faithful of all her servants, to discourse with him about their marriage.

THE OVERSEER BEATEN

And it came to pass, in those days, when Moses was grown, he went out unto his brethren, and looked on their burdens. And he spied an Egyptian smiting a Hebrew, one of his brethren.

And he looked this way and that way, and when he saw that there was no man, he slew the Egyptian, and hid him in the sand . . . .

Now when Pharaoh heard this thing, he sought to slay Moses. But Moses fled from the face of Pharaoh, and dwelt in the land of Midian; and he sat down by a well.

AT THE WELL OF JETHRO

Now the priest of Midian had seven daughters;
and they came and drew water, and filled the troughs
to water their father's flock.
And the shepherds came and drove them away,
but Moses stood up and helped them, and watered
their flock.

JETHRO'S SEVEN DAUGHTERS

*And Jethro said to his daughters: Where is he?
Why is it that you have left the man? Call him, that
he may eat bread.*

    *And Moses was content to dwell with the man;
and he gave Moses Zipporah his daughter.*

    And she bare him a son.

MOSES TENDS THE FLOCK OF JETHRO

Now Moses kept the flock of Jethro, his father-in-law, the priest of Midian; and he led the flock to the backside of the desert, and came to the Mountain of God, even unto Horeb.

THE BURNING BUSH

And the angel of the Lord appeared unto Moses in a flame of fire out of the midst of a bush; and he looked, and behold, the bush burned with fire, and the bush was not consumed.

JOURNEY TO EGYPT

*And Moses took his wife and his sons and set them
upon an ass, and he returned to the land of Egypt. And
Moses took the rod of God in his hand.*

*And the Lord said unto Moses: When thou goest
to return into Egypt, see that thou do all those wonders
before Pharaoh, which I have put in thine hand . . . .*

THE HEBREWS FORCED TO GATHER STRAW

*And Moses and Aaron went in and said to Pharaoh:
Thus saith the Lord God of Israel: Let my people go, that
they may hold a feast unto me in the wilderness.*

*And Pharaoh said: Who is the Lord that I should obey
his voice? . . . I know not the Lord, neither will I let Israel
go . . . .*

*And Pharaoh commanded the same day the taskmasters
of the people, and their officers, saying: You shall no more
give the people straw to make brick, as heretofore; let them
go and gather straw for themselves.*

AND GOD SPAKE UNTO MOSES

And God spake unto Moses, and said unto him: I am the Lord . . . .

And I appeared unto Abraham, Isaac, and Jacob, by the name of God Almighty, but by my name ADONAI was I not known to them.

I have established my covenant with them, to give them the land of Canaan, the land of their pilgrimage.

And I have also heard the groaning of the children of Israel, whom the Egyptians keep in bondage; and I have remembered my covenant.

MOSES WARNS PHARAOH

*And the Lord spake unto Moses, saying: Go
in, speak unto Pharaoh, king of Egypt, that he let
the children of Israel go out of his land.*

AARON'S ROD TURNS INTO A SERPENT

And the Lord spake unto Moses and unto Aaron, saying: When Pharaoh shall speak unto you, saying: Shew a miracle for you, then thou shalt say unto Aaron, Take thy rod, and cast it before Pharaoh, and it shall become a serpent.

And Moses and Aaron went in unto Pharaoh, and they did so as the Lord had commanded; and Aaron cast down his rod before Pharaoh, and before his servants, and it became a serpent.

THE PLAGUE OF FROGS

*And the Lord spake unto Moses: Say unto Aaron,
Stretch forth thine hand with thy rod over the streams,
over the rivers, and over the ponds, and cause frogs to
come up upon the land of Egypt.*

*And Aaron stretched out his hand over the waters
of Egypt; and the frogs came up and covered the land
of Egypt . . . .*

*Then Pharaoh called for Moses and Aaron, and
said: Intreat the Lord, that he may take away the frogs
from me, and from my people; and I will let the people
go, that they may do sacrifice unto the Lord.*

THE PLAGUE OF LICE

But when Pharaoh saw that there was respite, he hardened his heart, and hearkened not unto them, as the Lord had said.

And the Lord said unto Moses: Say unto Aaron, stretch out thy rod, and smite the dust of the land, that it may become lice throughout all the land of Egypt.

And they did so; Aaron stretched out his hand with his rod, and smote the dust of the earth, and it became lice upon man, and upon beast; all the dust of the land became lice throughout all the land of Egypt.

RAIN OF HAIL

And the Lord said unto Moses: Rise up early in the morning, and stand before Pharaoh, and say unto him, thus saith the Lord, God of the Hebrews; let my people go, that they may serve me . . . .

Behold, tomorrow about this time I will cause it to rain a very grievous hail, such as hath not been in Egypt since the foundation thereof even unto now.

DARKNESS OVER EGYPT

But the Lord hardened Pharaoh's heart, so that he would not let the children of Israel go.

And the Lord said unto Moses: Stretch out thine hand toward heaven, that there may be darkness over the land of Egypt, even darkness which may be felt.

And Moses stretched forth his hand toward heaven; and there was a thick darkness in all the land of Egypt three days.

MOSES AND AARON ADDRESS THE ISRAELITES

And the Lord spake unto Moses and Aaron in the land of Egypt, saying: . . . .

Speak ye unto all the congregation of Israel, saying, In the tenth day of this month they shall take to them every man a lamb, according to the house of their fathers, a lamb for a house.

EXODUS FROM EGYPT

And the Lord called for Moses and Aaron by night,
and said: Rise up, and get ye forth, from among my people,
both ye and the children of Israel; and go, serve the Lord,
as ye have said.

Also take your flocks and your herds, as ye have said,
and be gone; and bless me also . . . .

And it came to pass the selfsame day, that the Lord
did bring the children of Israel out of the land of Egypt . . . .

DROWNING OF THE EGYPTIANS

And the Lord said unto Moses: Stretch out thine hand over the sea, that the waters may come again upon the Egyptians, upon their chariots, and upon their horsemen . . . .

And the waters returned, and covered the chariots, and the horsemen, and all the host of Pharaoh that came into the sea after them; there remained not so much as one of them.

SONG OF VICTORY

Then sang Moses and the children of Israel this song unto the Lord, and spake, saying: I will sing unto the Lord for he has triumphed gloriously; the horse and his rider has he thrown into the sea.

MIRIAM AND THE WOMEN CELEBRATE

And Miriam the prophetess, the sister of Aaron, took a timbrel in her hand; and all the women went out after her with timbrels and with dances.

And Miriam said: Sing to the Lord, for he has triumphed gloriously; the horse and his rider has he thrown into the sea.

MOSES AND THE PEOPLE AT MARAH

*So Moses brought Israel from the Red Sea, and
they went out into the wilderness of Shur; and they
went three days in the wilderness, and found no water.*

*And when they came to Marah, they could not
drink of the waters of Marah, for they were bitter;
therefore, the name of it was called Marah.*

*And the people murmured against Moses, saying:
What shall we drink?*

*And he cried unto the Lord; and the Lord shewed
him a tree, and he had cast it into the waters, and the
waters were made sweet. . . .*

QUAILS ARRIVE FOR SUSTENANCE

And the Lord spake unto Moses, saying: I have heard the murmurings of the children of Israel; speak unto them, saying: At even ye shall eat flesh and in the morning ye shall be filled with bread; and ye shall know that I am the Lord your God.

And it came to pass, that at even the quails came up, and covered the camp; and in the morning the dew lay round about the camp.

THE STRIKING OF THE ROCK

There was no water for the people to drink. And the people murmured against Moses . . . .

And the Lord said unto Moses: Go on before the people, and take with thee of the elders of Israel; and thy rod, wherewith thou smotest the river, take in thy hand, and go.

Behold, I will stand before thee there upon the rock in Horeb; and thou shalt smite the rock, and there shall come water out of it, that the people may drink. And Moses did so . . . .

THE RAISED HAND OF MOSES

Then came Amalek, and fought with Israel in Rephidim.

And Moses said unto Joshua: Choose men, and go out, fight with Amalek. Tomorrow I will stand on the top of the hill with the rod of God in my hand.

So Joshua did as Moses had said to him, and fought with Amalek; and Moses, Aaron and Hur went up to the top of the hill.

And it came to pass, when Moses held up his hand, that Israel prevailed; and when he let down his hand, Amalek prevailed.

But Moses' hands were heavy . . . and Aaron and Hur held up his hands, the one on the one side, and the other on the other side; and his hands were steady until the going down of the sun.

REVENGE ON THE AMALEKITES

And Joshua discomfited Amalek and his people
with the edge of his sword.

And the Lord said unto Moses: Write this for
a memorial in a book and rehearse it in the ears of
Joshua; for I will utterly blot out the remembrance
of Amalek from under heaven.

JETHRO ADVISES MOSES TO CHOOSE JUDGES

*And it came to pass . . . that Moses sat to judge
the people; and the people stood by Moses from morning unto evening.*

*And when Moses' father-in-law saw all that he
did . . . he said: What is this thing that you do to the
people? Why do you sit alone, and all the people
stand from morning unto even? . . . .*

*Hearken now unto my voice, I will give you
counsel, and God shall be with you.*

*You shall provide out of all the people able men,
such as fear God, men of truth, hating covetousness. . . .*

*And let them judge the people at all seasons. And
it shall be that every great matter they shall bring unto
you, but every small matter they shall judge . . . .*

*So Moses hearkened to the voice of his father-in-
law, and did all that he had said.*

MOSES ASCENDS MOUNT SINAI

In the third month, when the children of Israel were gone forth out of the land of Egypt, the same day came they into the wilderness of Sinai. . . .

And Moses went up unto God, and the Lord called unto him out of the mountain, saying: Thus shalt thou say to the house of Jacob, and tell the children of Israel, Ye have seen what I did unto the Egyptians, and how I bare you on eagles' wings, and brought you unto myself.

Now therefore, if ye will obey my voice indeed, and keep my covenant, then ye shall be a treasure unto me above all people, for all the earth is mine.

And ye shall be unto me a kingdom of priests, and a holy nation. These are the words which thou shalt speak unto the children of Israel.

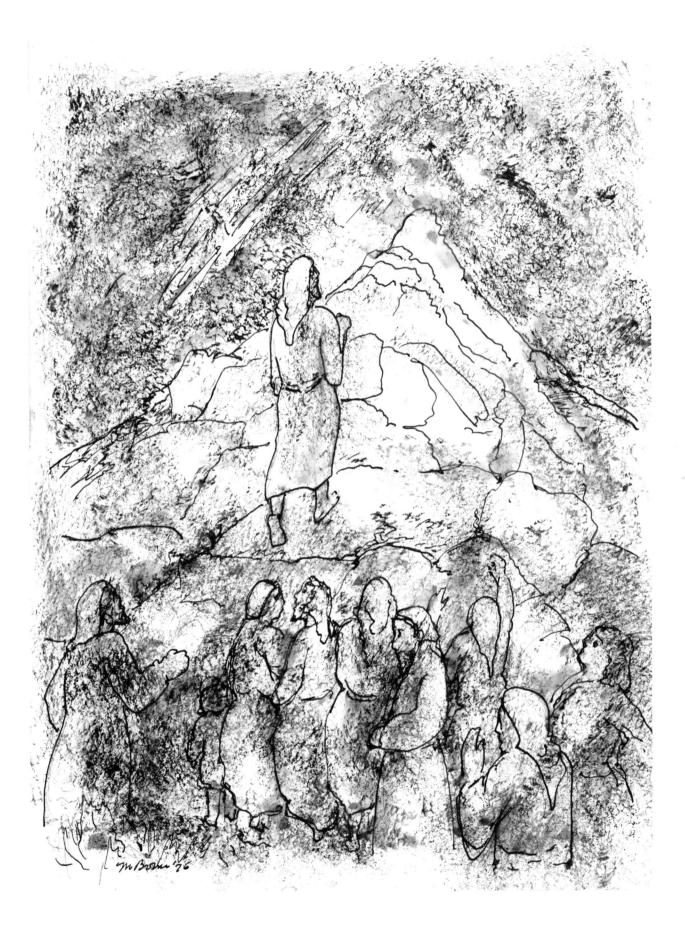

GOD SPAKE ALL THESE WORDS

*And God spake all these words, saying: I am the
Lord thy God, which have brought thee out of the
land of Egypt, out of the house of bondage. . . .
Thou shalt have no other gods before me.
Thou shalt not make unto thee any graven image. . . .
Thou shalt not take the name of the Lord thy God
in vain. . . .
Remember the sabbath day, to keep it holy, Six
days shalt thou labor and do all thy work.
Honor thy father and thy mother.
Thou shalt not murder.
Thou shalt not commit adultery.
Thou shalt not steal.
Thou shalt not bear false witness against thy neighbor.
Thou shalt not covet thy neighbor's house, thou shalt
not covet thy neighbor's wife, nor his manservant, nor
his maidservant, nor his ox, nor his ass, nor anything
that is thy neighbor's.*

MOSES BRINGS THE LAW

And Moses came and told the people all the words of the Lord, and all the judgements; and all the people answered with one voice, and said: All the words which the Lord hath said will we do. . . .

And Moses took the book of the covenant, and read in the hearing of the people; and they said: All that the Lord hath said will we do, and be obedient.

THE CHOOSING OF THE PRIESTS

And the Lord said: Take thou unto thee Aaron
thy brother, and his sons with him from among the
children of Israel that he may minister unto me in
the priest's office, even Aaron, Nadab and Abihu,
Eleazar and Ithamar, Aaron's sons.

And thou shalt make holy garments for Aaron,
thy brother, for glory and for beauty.

And thou shalt speak unto all that are wise-
hearted, whom I have filled with the spirit of wisdom,
that they may make Aaron's garments to consecrate
him, that he may minister unto me in the priest's
office. . . .

AARON AS HIGH PRIEST

*And thou shalt take the garments and put upon
Aaron the coat, and the robe of the ephod, and the
ephod, and the breast-plate, and gird him with the
curious girdle of the ephod.*

BEZALEEL CREATES WORKS IN METAL STONE AND WOOD

And the Lord spake unto Moses, saying: See, I have called by name Bezaleel the son of Uri, the son of Hur, of the tribe of Judah.

And I have filled him with the spirit of God, in wisdom, and in understanding, and in knowledge and in all manner of workmanship;

To devise cunning works, to work in gold, and in silver, and in brass, and in cutting of stones, to set them, and in carving of timber, to work in all manner of workmanship.

THE GOLDEN CALF

*And when the people saw that Moses delayed
to come down from the mount, the people gathered
themselves together unto Aaron, and said to him:
Make us gods , which shall go before us.*

*As for this Moses, the man that brought us up
out of the land of Egypt, we know not what is become
of him.*

*And Aaron said unto them: Take off the golden
earrings, which are in the ears of your wives, of your
sons, and of your daughters, and bring them to me.*

*And all the people took off the golden earrings
which were in their ears, and brought them to Aaron.*

*And he received them at their hand, and fashion-
ed them in a mould, and made a molten calf. And they
said: These are your gods, O Israel, which brought you
out of the land of Egypt.*

MOSES BREAKS THE TABLETS

And it came to pass, as soon as Moses came nigh unto the camp, that he saw the calf, and the dancing; and Moses' anger waxed hot, and he cast the tablets out of his hands, and broke them beneath the mount.

And he took the calf which they had made, and burnt it in the fire, and ground it to powder, and strewed it upon the water, and made the children of Israel drink of it.

And Moses said unto Aaron: What did this people unto you that you have brought so great a sin upon them?

THE LAWS BROUGHT AGAIN

And the Lord said unto Moses: Hew thee two
tablets of stone like unto the first; and I will write
upon these tablets the words that were in the first
tablets, which thou breakest.

And be ready in the morning, and come up in
the morning unto Mount Sinai, and present thyself
there to me in the top of the mount. . . .

And the Lord said unto Moses: Write thou
these words, for after the tenor of these words I
have made a covenant with thee and with Israel.

And he was there with the Lord forty days and
forty nights; he did neither eat bread, nor drink water.
And he wrote upon the tablets the words of the covenant, the ten commandments.

MOSES SPEAKS TO THE CHILDREN OF ISRAEL

And the Lord spake unto Moses, saying: Speak unto all the congregation of the children of Israel, and say unto them, Ye shall be holy, for I the Lord your God am holy.

Ye shall fear every man his mother, and his father, and keep my sabbaths; I am the Lord your God.

Turn ye not unto idols, nor make to yourselves molten gods; I am the Lord your God. . . .

And when you reap the corners of thy field, neither shalt thou gather the gleanings of thy harvest.

And thou shalt not glean thy vineyard, neither shalt thou gather every grape of thy vineyard; thou shalt leave them for the poor and stranger; I am the Lord your God. . . .

REVOLT AGAINST MOSES

Now Korah, the son of Izhar, the son of Kehath,
the son of Levi, and Dathan and Abiram, the sons of
Eliab, and On, the son of Peleth, sons of Reuben, took
courage.

And they rose up before Moses, with certain of
the children of Israel, two hundred and fifty princes
of the congregation, those convoked to the assembly,
men of renown.

And they gathered themselves together against
Moses and against Aaron, and said unto them: You
take too much upon you, seeing all the congregation
are holy, every one of them, and the Lord is among
them; wherefore then lift you up yourselves above the
congregation of the Lord?

THE DEMISE OF KORAH AND HIS MEN

And the Lord spake unto Moses, saying: Speak
unto the congregation, saying, get you up from about
the tabernacle of Korah, Dathan and Abiram. . . .

And he spake unto the congregation, saying:
Depart, I pray you, from the tents of these wicked men,
and touch nothing of theirs, lest you be consumed in
all their sins.

So they got up from the tabernacle of Korah,
Dathan, and Abiram, on every side. . . .

And Moses said: Hereby you shall know that the
Lord has sent me to do all these works; for I have not
done them of mine own mind. . . .

And it came to pass, as he had made an end of
speaking all these words, that the ground under them
clave asunder.

And the earth opened her mouth, and swallowed
them up and their houses, and all the men that apper-
tained unto Korah, and all their goods.

KORAH'S FOLLOWERS SWALLOWED BY THE EARTH

BALAAM AND THE ASS

And Balaam said unto God: Balak the son of
Zippor, king of Moab, has sent unto me, saying:
Behold there is a people come out of Egypt, which
covereth the face of the earth; come now, curse them;
peradventure I shall be able to overcome them, and
drive them out.

And God said unto Balaam: Thou shalt not go
with them; thou shalt not curse the people, for they
are blessed. . . .

Now Balaam rose up in the morning, and saddled
his ass and went with the princes of Moab.

And God's anger was kindled because he went; and
the angel of the Lord stood in the way for an adversary
against him. . . .

And the ass saw the angel of the Lord standing in
the way, and his sword drawn in his hand; and the ass
turned aside out of the way. . . . and Balaam smote the
ass, to turn her into the way. . . .

And Balaam said unto the angel of the Lord: I have
sinned. . . . . now therefore, if it pleases you, I will get
me back again.

THE DAUGHTERS OF MOAB

*And Israel abode in Shittim, and the people began
to commit whoredom with the daughters of Moab.*

*And they called the people unto the sacrifices of
their gods; and the people did eat, and bowed down
to their gods.*

*And Israel joined himself unto Baal-peor; and the
anger of the Lord was kindled against Israel.*

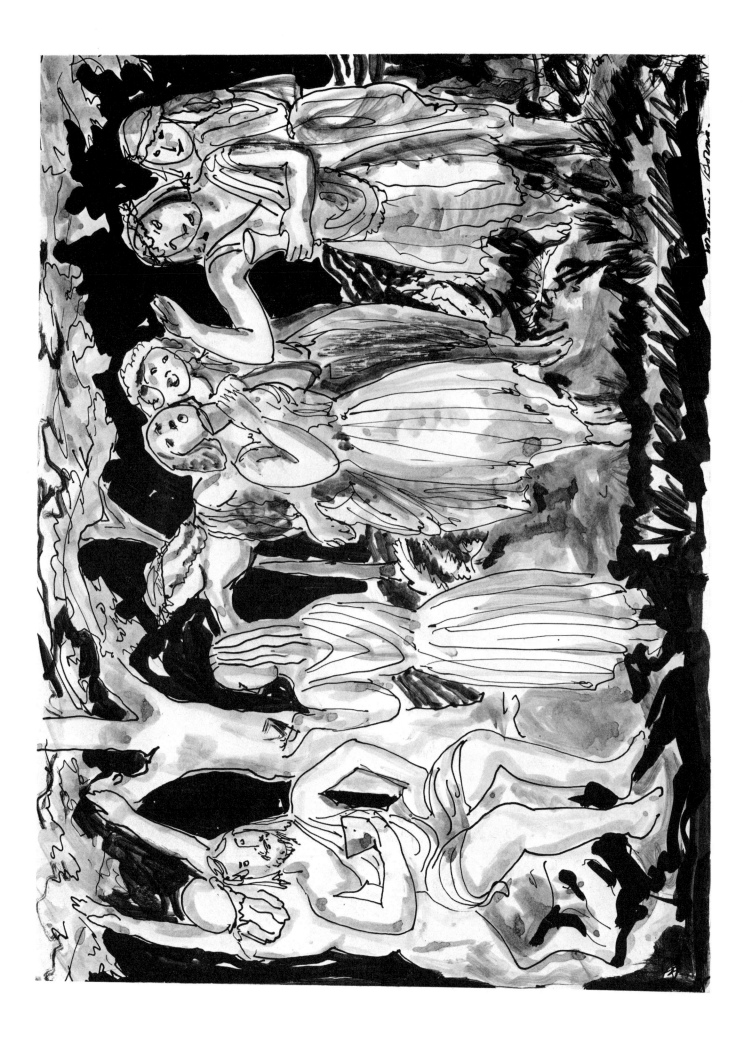

MOSES TURNS OVER THE COMMAND
TO JOSHUA

And Moses went and spake these words unto all Israel.

And he said unto them: I am a hundred and twenty years old this day; I can no more go out and come in; also the Lord has said to me, Thou shalt not go over this Jordan. . . .

And Moses called unto Joshua, and said to him: Be strong and of a good courage, for you must go with this people unto the land which the Lord has sworn unto their fathers to give them, and you shall cause them to inherit it.

And the Lord, he it is that goes before you; he will be with you, he will not fail you. neither forsake you; fear not, neither be dismayed. . . .

MOSES AND JOSHUA

And the Lord said unto Moses: Behold, thy days approach that thou must die. Call Joshua . . . that I may give him a charge. . . .

And he gave Joshua the son of Nun a charge, and said: Be strong and of a good courage, for thou shalt bring the children of Israel into the land which I sware unto them; and I will be with thee.

MOSES BEHOLDS THE LAND OF CANAAN

*And the Lord spake unto Moses that selfsame
day, saying: Get thee up into this mountain Abirim,
unto Mount Nebo, which is in the land of Moab, that
is over against Jericho; and behold the land of Canaan,
which I give unto the children of Israel for possession.*

DEATH OF MOSES

So Moses, the servant of the Lord, died there in the land of Moab, according to the word of the Lord.

And he was buried in a valley in the land of Moab, over against Beth-peor; but no man knoweth of his sepulchre unto this day.

And Moses was a hundred and twenty years old when he died; his eye was not dim, nor his vigor abated.

And the children of Israel wept for Moses, in the plains of Moab thirty days; so the days of weeping and mourning for Moses were ended.

EPILOGUE: FALL OF THE WALLS OF JERICHO

After the death of Moses, Joshua and the people of Israel moved on toward the land of Canaan. Here they captured a number of cities and came to Jericho, a town fortified by walls, located about fifteen miles northeast of Jerusalem.

Joshua and the people circled the city many times with blowing of trumpets, and at a given signal by Joshua, all the people gave out a thundering shout, and the walls of Jericho came tumbling down.

. . . "So Joshua took the whole land, according to all that the Lord had said unto Moses; and Joshua gave it for an inheritance unto Israel" (Joshua 12: 23).